Hey

Foreword

What strikes us first, when we look at the body of work created by Hey, is a love for what they do. They say, 'if you love what you do, then you will never work another day in your life', and I think there is certainly some truth to that old adage. To that effect, it is clear why Hey have picked up a cult-like status among their hundreds of thousands of social media fans, during their ten years in design.

Everything we love about design is celebrated within their work; from colour, shape and pattern to illustration and typography – these disparate elements, continuously intertwining to amaze, delight and enthrall us.

The Barcelona-based studio is renowned for its bright, playful graphics and their output is a fine example of what can be achieved, with a limited number of graphic devices, in order to bring about a strikingly arresting end result. They contrast and clash shapes and colours, while forms are bent, ripped and manoeuvred in endless ways – always culminating in something fresh; something new.

There is a sense of creativity within their work, and indeed of play, alongside unquestionable technical ability. Their work, much like their name, is fun. We never view a Hey project that appears not to have been a joy to create and this is due, in part, to the fact that many of their projects stem from personal work and the same sense of energy is present in both. It is this sense of balance between commercial work and experimental projects that has garnered so many fans, many of whom would surely dream of enjoying a similar level of creative freedom.

One of the things that drew me to the work of Hey, from early on in their career, was the seamless marriage of design and illustration – as completely fresh ten years ago as it is today. This potent mix has resulted in an enviable client list, including the likes of Paypal, Nokia and Oxfam.

The work on show within this book, from clients such as these as well as the promotional pieces and illustrations, is by no means a complete archive of Hey's work. Neither is it exclusively the prize-winning or the most 'well-known' projects. The work was selected primarily to demonstrate the versatility of the studio's output and the written text included in order to explain how Hey confront design problems; how ideas are hatched and problems solved.

Though the studio's output has been studied, exhibited and honoured within the international graphic arts community, much of this work is published for the first time.

Hey is equally well-known in Europe for its illustrative work for the likes of Monocle, the global affairs and lifestyle magazine, as they are for creating brand identities for some of the bastions of Spanish design. Organisations such as ADC and CCCB are clients that Hey have worked with for many years and brand identity is a critical part of the studio's output.

Hey's graphic and branding work is characterised by the juxtaposition of bold geometric shapes, a riot of colour and the clever use of materials. These playful concepts are then realised with strong, clean typography – the mix of regimented grids and illustrative graphics, creating inventive and exciting solutions.

The woman that has coordinated, championed, crafted and carried the Hey banner for over ten years is Verònica Fuerte. Fuerte set up the studio in 2007, after several years spent working for a variety of design studios in Barcelona. Over time, she has built Hey into the multi-disciplinary studio that it is today, currently a five person team. As their notoriety has grown, so has their client list; with larger names jumping on-board, including the likes of Apple, Wall Street Journal, and Penguin/Random House – all seduced by their bold, brightly-coloured, forward-thinking design work.

Hey are one of the most innovative design agencies of recent years and regardless of what medium or field they work in, it is clear that we are all discovering a group of creatives who clearly unite both spheres of design and illustration with ingenuity, warmth and wit. For the name 'Hey', is not only a moniker for the company, but an ethos – a smile, a surprise, a welcome shock to the system – and every form of communication that comes out of their studio adheres to this. That sense of fun has become synonymous with their design projects, illustrations and even their working environment.

We hope that this book reflects this. It is a book for anyone interested in visual communication and, above all, creativity. It is for professionals and students, executives of large corporations and managers of small businesses, art directors and everyone else curious about Hey and the world of graphic design and illustration.

Jon Dowling
Counter-Print

Patterns

Arrels

2015–2017

Arrels, which means 'roots' in English, is a Barcelona-based footwear brand, making shoes for the urban market.

For Hey, creating the identity meant, 'finding the right balance between their urban look and their rural roots' and between, 'being handmade and mass-produced'.

This duality is reflected in the two colours of the identity and in the pattern created for the boxes and the shoes; an idea which was carried over to the brochure.

The design of the pattern plays with the idea that if you were to rip up all the layers of concrete which cover the urban landscape underneath your feet, you would find the original, natural surface of the earth.

Creating the identity meant finding the right balance between their urban look and their rural roots and between being handmade and mass produced.

2015 ↗
Pattern design for Arrels.

2015
Identity and marketing
materials for Arrels.

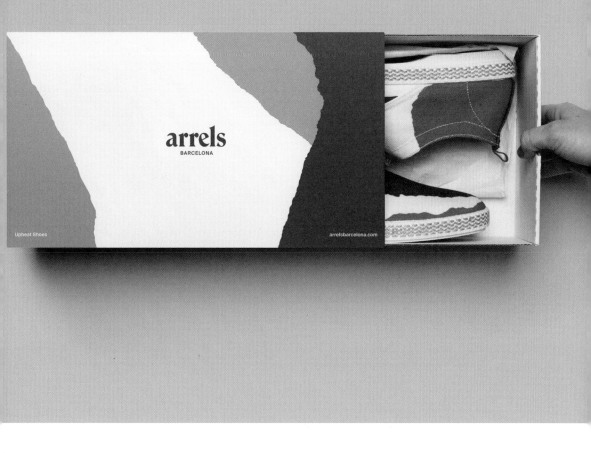

2015
Shoe box design.

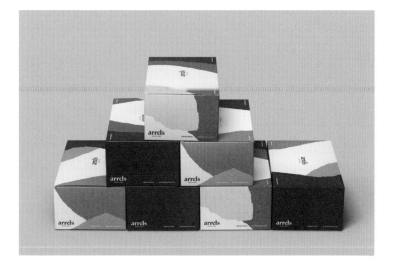

2015
Arrels brandbook.

FEET ON THE
GROUND,
HEAD IN THE
CLOUDS

...d shoemakers second;
...ove to innovate.
...experiment with shoes.
...lections together with
...s, graphic designers,
... over the details with
...isan because it is the
...we enjoy above all else.
...ore? No, like kids in

MALIKA FAVRE

Sober elegance. Post minimalism. Pop Art combined with Op Art. Malika's style is personal, unique and almost impossible to catalogue. The only two words that could actually be used to define it are: Malika Favre. What is unquestionable is that this London-based French artist is one of the most respected visual artists in Europe. Her portfolio includes The New Yorker, Vogue, and BAFTA, among many others.

2018
Packaging design for
Caravelle's own-brand
beer labels.

Caravelle

2018

Caravelle, based in the Raval neighbourhood of central Barcelona, is a restaurant that caters for a wide range of modern tastes: dining, brunch, smokehouse, specialty coffees and, their latest addition, a nano brewery.

At the end of 2017 they were looking to expand the branding of their craft beer which they brew on-site. Hey's aim was to create a visual branding and conceptual system: a single generic label, with clear Caravelle branding, that could be used for each label in the planned range of six beers.

Hey created a revitalised branding, utilising a series of landscapes made from layers of gradients. These labels came in varying colour palettes, depicting the seasons.

Caravelle
Galactic IPA
Caravelle
Electric Relaxation XPA
Caravelle
Grand Pacific Kölsch

Film Commission Chile

2011

The Film Commission Chile (FCCh) was created to promote Chile as a movie production destination, to help in choosing locations, to provide a variety of services and a link between government and private companies.

FCCh's visual identity is inspired by duct/gaffer tape, as the tape is omnipresent in the world of movie production. Tape is used to unite, join, mark, hold, point, remind and help. Due to its flexibility, the lines and shape of the tape also resemble the classic movie celluloid film. This graphic device is manipulated in different directions, creating a dynamic universe that conceptually represents FCCh's linking mission.

The variations in the colour palette are described by Hey as being representative of, 'the diversity of landscapes we can find in the Chilean territory'. All elements combined, compose a unique image, with a well-defined personality, perfectly adapted to the objectives of the FCCh.

Tapes unite, join, mark, hold, point, remind and help. Due to its flexibility, the lines and shape of the tape also resemble the classic movie celluloid film.

2011 ↗
Identity design for The
Film Commission Chile.

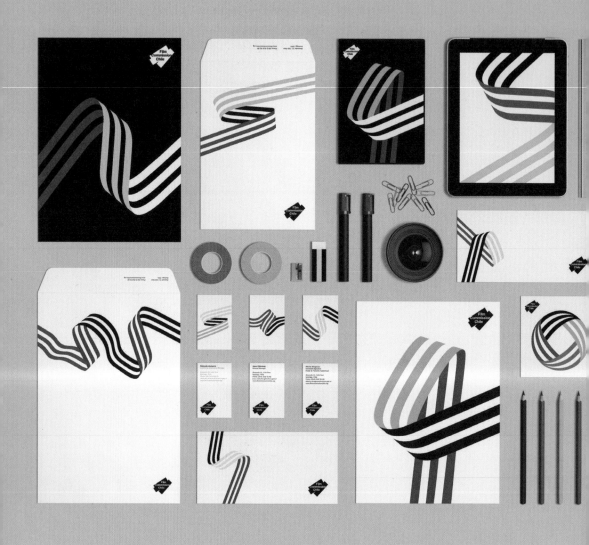

The variations in the colour palette are described by Hey as being representative of, 'the diversity of landscapes we can find in the Chilean territory'.

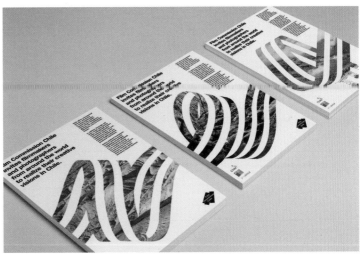

2011
Identity design for The Film Commission Chile.

Camping is an urban chiringuito.
The design for its identity is based
on the classic Mediterranean
blue and white stripes but with
a refreshing twist.

2019
Identity design for
Camping, an urban
chiringuito.

2013
Identity for Generalitat
de Catalunya.

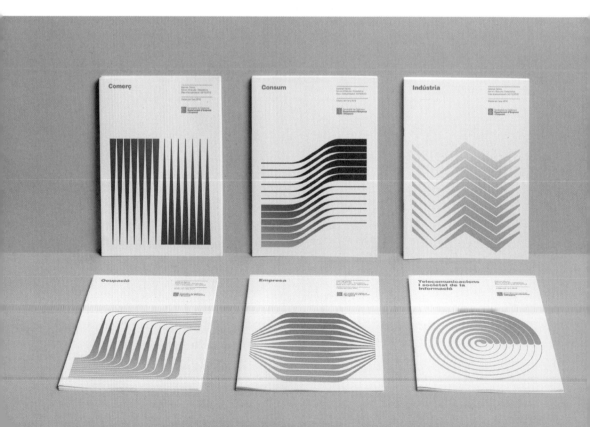

**Mercat
de treball**

Demandes d'ocupació
Atur registrat
Contractació laboral

Dades del l'any 2008

Gabinet Tècnic
Servei d'Estudis i Estadística
Data d'actualització: 02/12/2008

Generalitat de Catalunya
Departament de Treball

Observatori
del Treball

Dones

Anuari Dones i Treball

Dades del l'any 2008

Gabinet Tècnic
Servei d'Estudis i Estadística
Data d'actualització: 02/12/2008

Generalitat de Catalunya
Departament de Treball

**Visió
transversal i
multitemàtica**

Estadística de l'Enquesta
de conjuntada laboral

Dades del l'any 2008

Gabinet Tècnic
Servei d'Estudis i Estadística
Data d'actualització: 02/12/2008

Generalitat de Catalunya
Departament de Treball

Observatori
del Treball

**Població
estrangera**

Població activa
Ocupació
Contractació laboral
Atur

Dades del l'any 2008

Gabinet Tècnic
Servei d'Estudis i Estadística
Data d'actualització: 02/12/2008

Generalitat de Catalunya
Departament de Treball

MACBA

2018

The Museum of Contemporary Art of Barcelona (MACBA) is one of the city's leading cultural institutions, an iconic architectural symbol as well as a reference point for art and culture. In the spring of 2018, UNIQLO, the global Japanese clothing company, who had recently arrived in the city, became their official partner.

 The partnership gave free entry to the museum every Saturday evening and invited people to participate in activities such as the 'Let's talk about art' guided visits and the 'Late MACBA session'.

 Hey were commissioned to create a campaign that represented the close relationship between the two big institutions in the city centre. Under the umbrella of the 'Dissabtes MACBA' (MACBA's Saturdays) campaign name, created by Nom-Nam, Hey developed a bold visual strategy that physically represented the merging of both brands.

 The square logotypes of MACBA and UNIQLO are brought together into coloured shapes that always connect, showing that this new initiative was only feasible thanks to both brands coming together. The palette is limited to the colours of both brands, black and red, to emphasise the fusion of two institutions into a unique entity.

 The system was applied across different formats, from posters and bus ads to digital screens in the museum.

The square logotypes of MACBA and UNIQLO are brought together into coloured shapes that always connect, showing that this new initiative was only feasible thanks to both brands coming together.

2018 ↗
Campaign for Dissabtes
MACBA x UNIQLO.

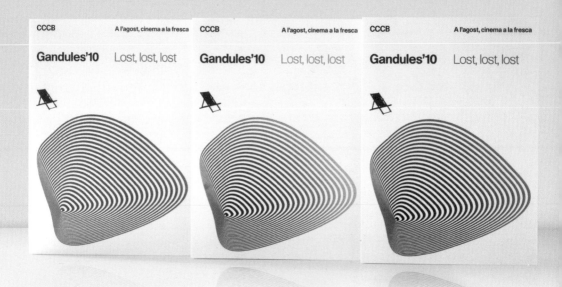

2010
Design of CCCB's 2010
open air cinema season
'Gandules'.

2011 ↗
Design of Gandules 2011.

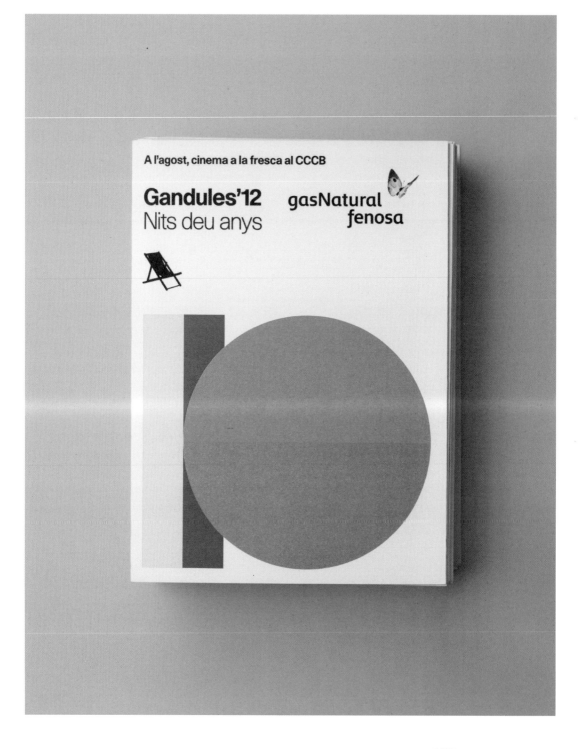

2012
Design of Gandules
2012.

2013 ↗
Design of Gandules
2013.

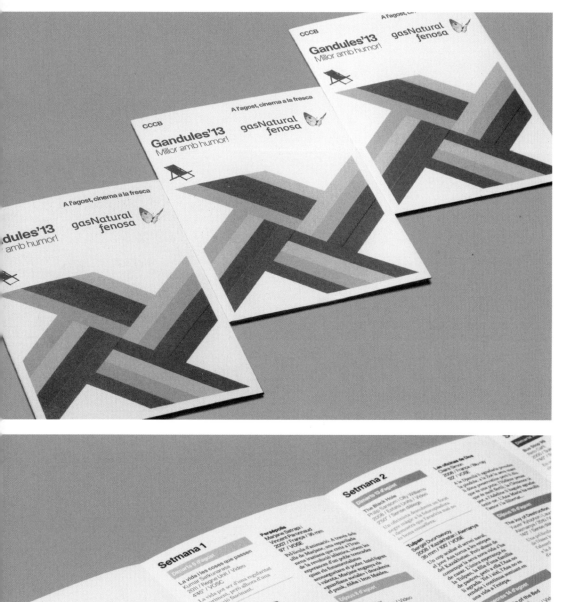

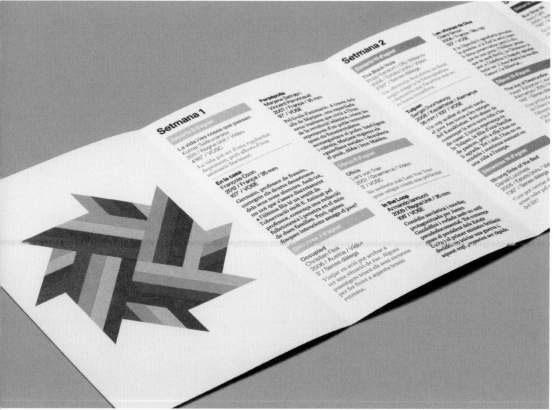

Global gay

Frédéric Martel

Cómo la revolución gay
está cambiando el mundo

taurus
T

↖ 2013
Book design for Taurus
editorial.

2012
Self-promotional
Christmas poster for Hey.

Ajuntament de Barcelona

2017

Christmas in Barcelona not only sees a big increase in consumer spending but also in the cultural and social events that take place. In recent years the city council has chosen to reflect the full range of these festive activities, rather than just focus on the commercial side of the holidays. They have done this by taking a more narrative approach to their campaigns.

The administration got in touch with Hey and gave the studio the task of devising the concept and creative approach for the city's 2017 Christmas campaign. The communication required a tone which was not only friendly and festive but which also had to convey the idea of, 'coexistence, participation and togetherness'. They wanted it to be 'fresh' and 'modern' and to move away from the more 'conventional' festive themes.

Hey worked with Usted to come up with the concept for the campaign. The idea was to reinforce the message that Barcelona is an open and tolerant city, a place where there isn't a right way to celebrate Christmas but instead somewhere where everyone can do their own thing.

The campaign was aligned under the concept of 'Viu el teu Nadal' or 'Live your own Christmas'. Within all the elements of the campaign, Hey played with the idea of using elements that weren't normally associated with one another, feeling these obvious contrasts would make the campaign more interesting to the public. So, the copy written started with the type of traditional Christmas features and themes that you would expect but they then added an element which immediately looked out of place and clashed with the festive subject. This was in order to make the point that, no matter what plans or tastes a citizen has, they are welcome in Barcelona and the most important part of it – live Christmas the way you want to.

Hey used the striped lines to represent a diverse Barcelona. Red and green ribbons cover objects which have a universal Christmas appeal. Some of the items are traditionally festive but others are things from everyday life.

2017
Banner designs for
Ajuntament de Barcelona.

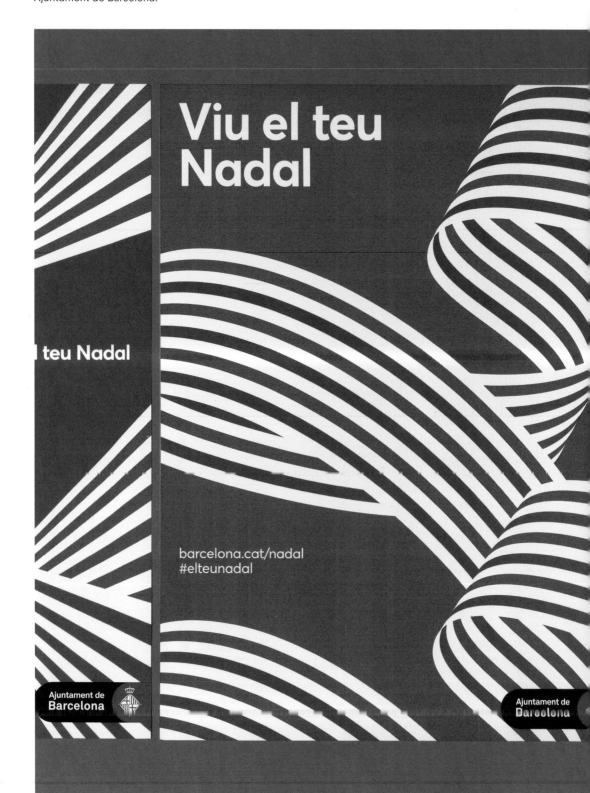

Perfums. Bufandes. Clavicordis.

A les botigues de barri hi ha regals
er a tots els gustos.

Viu el teu Nadal

barcelona.cat/nadal
#elteunadal

Espectacle

A la plaça
variades pe

Viu el teu N

Del 22 de desemb
al 4 de gener

Ajuntament de
Barcelona

2019
'Let it Blow' poster to
celebrate the 2019 New
Year, in collaboration
with Andrés Reisinger.

The graphics for this packaging design were created using traditional marbling techniques, a process that produces random patterns where no two designs are the same.

2019
Packaging design for Daydream, a sparkling water infused with hemp extracts.

YG17

2019

The One Club For Creativity invited Hey to develop the identity of their Young Guns award (YG17), which recognises the vanguard of creative professionals 30 years of age and under. Founded in 1996, the portfolio-based competition has grown to become one of the most coveted awards for young creatives around the globe.

The identity is inspired by the event itself and how it puts the spotlight on young talent. Hey spent some time studying light and played with its behaviour as it passes through objects. Refractions, reflections and occlusions were the foundations they used in developing the identity.

Intersecting beams of light, colour contrasts and complete darkness make it a playful system, with a wide variety of solutions for every format, from static to animated.

2019
Identity for The One Club
For Creativity's Young Guns
award (YG17).

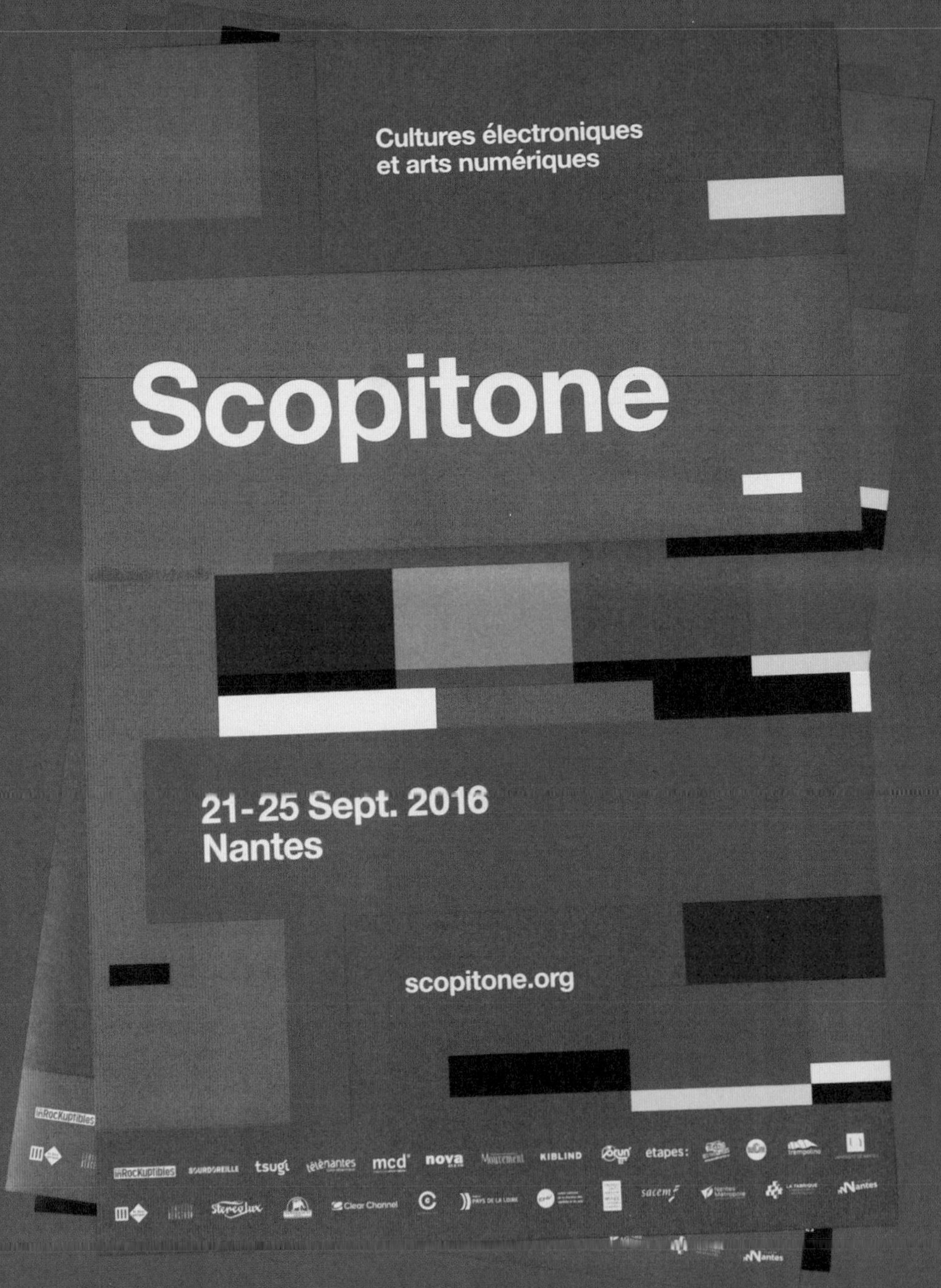

Cultures électroniques
et arts numériques

Scopitone

21-25 Sept. 2016
Nantes

scopitone.org

2020
'Burst' poster designed
to celebrate the 2020
New Year in collaboration
with Andrés Reisinger.

2021 ↗
'Marble' poster designed
to celebrate the 2021
New Year in collaboration
with Alex Trochut.

Fundació Joan Miró

2016

In 1957 the artist Joan Miró created a venue in Barcelona where his works of art could be researched and made available to a wider public. This space, the Fundació Joan Miró, contacted Hey in 2016 to design the visual identity for one of their temporary exhibitions. 'Endgame: Duchamp, Chess, and the Avant-Garde' reinterpreted modern art history through its relationship with chess. It ran for three months and exhibited works from numerous twentieth century artists.

Hey came up with a proposal where both the visual and conceptual focus was on avant-garde cubism. They played with the fragmentation of surfaces, echoing how cubist artists worked at the beginning of the twentieth century. Hey decided to combine graphic design with images from paintings in the exhibition, such as 'Simultaneous Dresses' by Sonia Delaunay or 'Motor, Laboratory of Ideas' by Jean Crotti.

Cubist masterpieces, in which a chessboard appears, were utilised so the studio could create new images, where the chess board runs through the painting and invades the work. Hey wanted to create a confusion between the artwork and the chessboard, in much the same way that Juan Gris and Fernand Léger did in their paintings. This approach also allowed Hey to create a flexible visual system, which could be adapted to numerous formats and sizes.

The design was applied to different materials, such as the exhibition poster, the opening invitations, the programme (in four languages) and the indoor signage.

Hey came up with a proposal where both the visual and conceptual focus was on avant-garde cubism.

2016
Identity for a temporary
exhibition at Fundació
Joan Miró.

FIN DE PARTIDA
DUCHAMP, EL AJEDREZ
Y LAS VANGUARDIAS

29.10.2016—22.01.2017

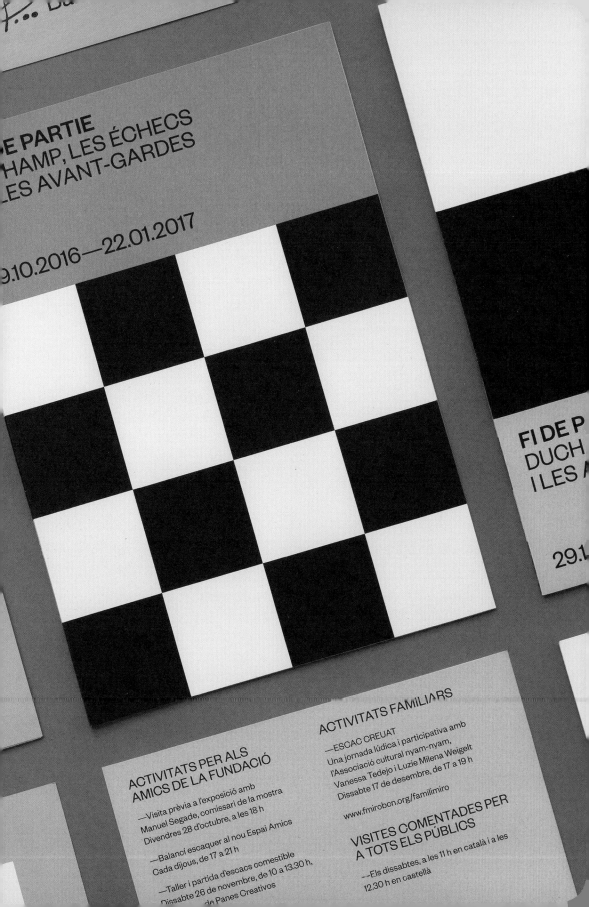

2014
Business cards
for Jammy Yummy.

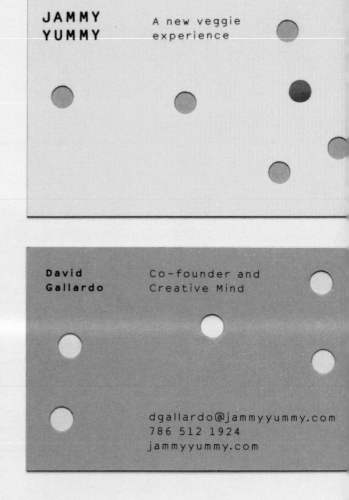

JAMMY YUMMY
A new veggie experience

David Gallardo
Co-founder and Creative Mind

dgallardo@jammyyummy.com
786 512 1924
jammyyummy.com

JAMMY YUMMY
A new veggie experience

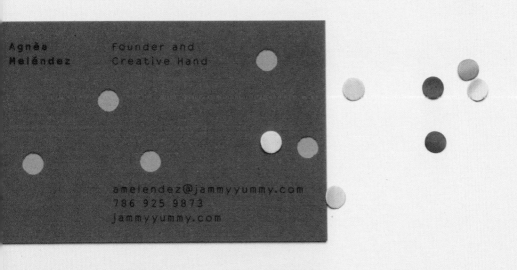

Agnès
Meléndez

founder and
Creative Hand

amelendez@jammyyummy.com
786 925 9873
jammyyummy.com

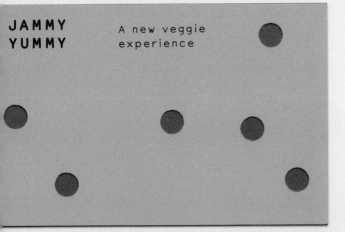

JAMMY
YUMMY

A new veggie
experience

Agnès
Meléndez

Founder and
Creative Hand

amelendez@jammyyummy.com
786 925 9873
jammyyummy.com

UNIQLO

2017

During the autumn of 2017, UNIQLO launched a new store in Barcelona. Typically, when UNIQLO open new stores in new countries they usually create shopping bags designed with the local culture in mind. For the opening of the new Barcelona store, Hey were asked to create three shopping bag designs and a mural for the store's interior.

Although UNIQLO are a global brand, they wished to spread the message that they respect and understand the city as it really is; not wanting to change things, but instead choosing to integrate. That is why Hey came up with the idea titled, 'Homes: the true identity of a city'.

A large number of Barcelona's citizens live in flats with beautiful antique floor tiles. This creative direction features this colourful flooring, which dates from the 19th century and remains incredibly popular today. As home is where people can be themselves and act freely, the public can visually connect this identity with their homes.

Three bag designs were created, that evoke classic antique floors.

2017
Poster and notebook
design for the
Independent Barcelona
Coffee Festival.

For its second edition, Hey was asked to create
the Independent Barcelona Coffee Festival's graphic
identity. The studio designed a boldly illustrated poster,
showing the essence of the festival – numerous cups
of coffee, ready to be served.

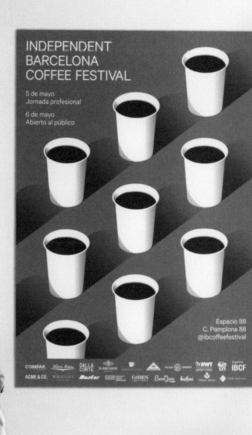

INDEPENDENT
BARCELONA
COFFEE FESTIVAL

5 de mayo
Jornada profesional

6 de mayo
Abierto al público

Espacio 88
C. Pamplona 88
@ibcoffeefestival

Shapes

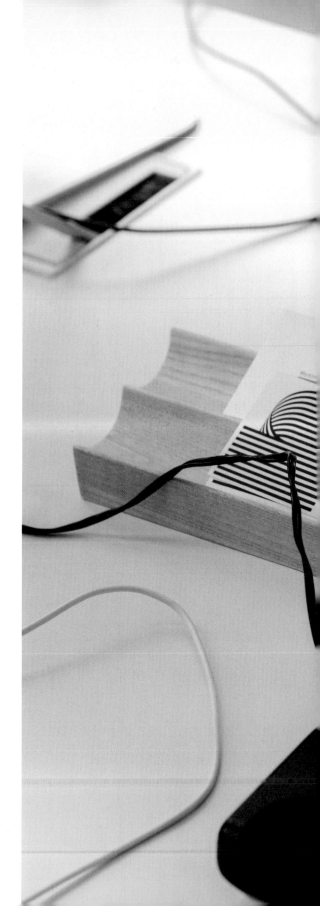

CCCB – Centre de Cultura Contemporània de Barcelona

2011–2018

Since 2011, Hey have carried out the design of the bi-monthly programme of events for the Barcelona Contemporary Art Centre (CCCB), a space for multi-disciplinary contemporary culture. The concept for the initial programme came out of seeing the museum as a receptacle for contemporary ideas. The square on the cover is the CCCB building, as seen from above, and the aim of the studio was to create a design that could last for five years without losing its appeal.

For the 2017–2018 iteration, Hey were asked to review their design. The CCCB were looking to refresh the design but wanted to retain continuity with the existing style. For the cover, Hey kept the idea of representing the shape of the building as a square but this time the form moves within the space and moves position from one piece of communication to another. This was executed to represent the busy and active nature of the institution, the multidisciplinary nature of their activities and the way they have evolved over the years.

Inside the leaflet a more flexible grid was created and the information laid out with a clearer hierarchy of categories.

The square on the cover is the CCCB building, as seen from above, and the aim of the studio was to create a design that could last for five years without losing its appeal.

2012 ↗
Design of the bi-monthly programme of events for CCCB, the Barcelona Contemporary Art Centre.

The concept came out of seeing the museum as a receptacle for contemporary ideas.

2013
Design of the bi-monthly
programme of events
for CCCB, the Barcelona
Contemporary Art Centre.

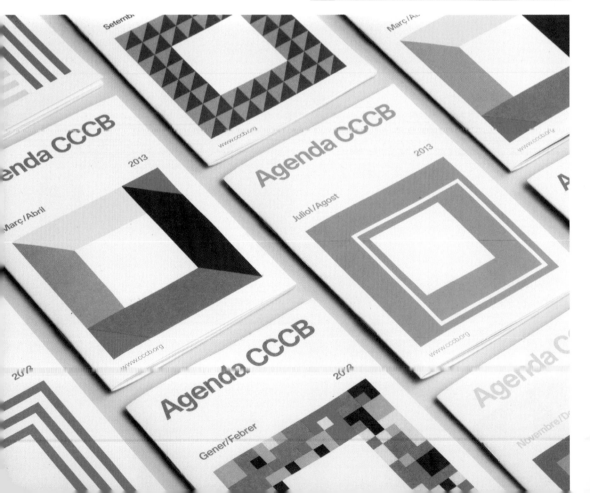

2017
Design refresh of the
bi-monthly programme
of events for CCCB.

CCCB

Agenda Maig/Juny 2017

CCCB

Agenda Mar/Abr 2017

CCCB

CCCB

Agenda Gen/Feb 2017

CCCB

Agenda Juliol/Agost 2017

CCCB

CCCB

Agenda Set/Oct 2017

Agenda Nov/Des 2017

2019
Design of the bi-monthly
programme of events
for CCCB, the Barcelona
Contemporary Art Centre.

2020 ↘
Exterior signage for the
reopening of CCCB after
the 2020 quarantine.

Andrew G

CEO / Lawy
a.giles@astor
+44 (0) 7786
astorgiles.com

dvocate
s.com
8 954

r Advocate
stor giles.com
) 7786 438 954
torgiles.com

↙ 2018
Identity for boutique law
firm Astor Giles.

2019
Wedding invitation design.

Hey's first ever wedding invitation
design is a graphic and abstract
representation of the marriage
between two people. Two circular
shapes come together and
perfectly fit to celebrate this
beautiful union.

2015
Identity for Barcelona
Gallery Weekend.

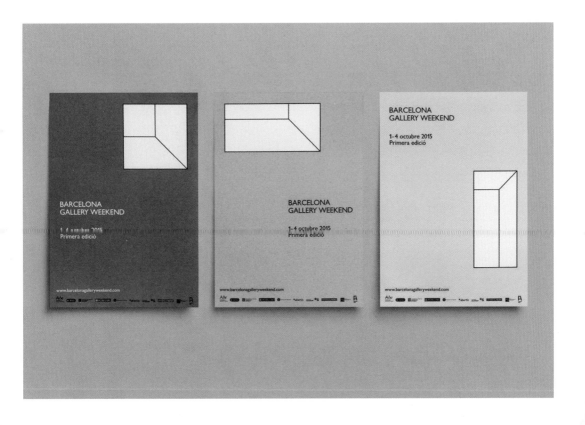

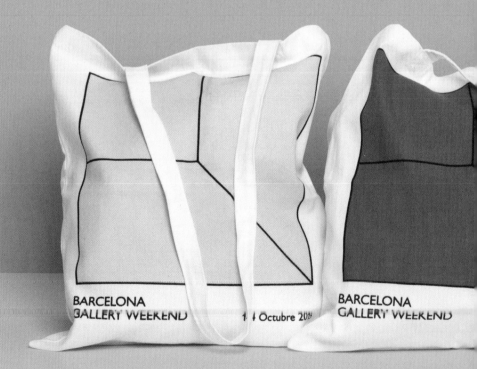

2017
Creative direction and
editorial design for the
white paper 'Blau sobre
Blanc', published by JNC.

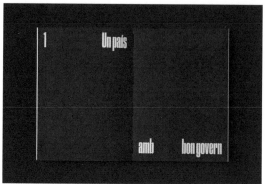

Joventut Nacionalista de Catalunya

2017

In 2017 JNC published a white paper, 'Blau sobre Blanc. Idees per la Catalunya Estat', which explored the idea of Catalonia as a new state. It brought together fifteen articles under five chapters, looking at different political, economical, cultural and social aspects. Each article contained two texts by different authors. One of which was always written by a member of the party.

Hey worked on the creative direction and editorial design for the publication. They created a book where the idea of the title was translated into something visual. Blue ink over white paper.

The content was divided into five chapters, containing the different articles and, to give a sense of flow and clarity in a 200+ page publication, the articles appeared using two different ink colours, black and blue. Blue, being JRC's colour, was always used for the party member's articles.

Laus 2010

2010

Hey were tasked with creating the identity for the Spanish Laus Design Awards which turned 40 in 2010. When the studio was initially asked to design the campaign, they were delighted as they saw it as a real challenge to create something for designers because all eyes would be on their work.

Hey developed an abstract campaign that reflected the passing of time. The 'L', that stands for 'Laus', was represented in a variety of coloured sheets of paper which were die-cut.

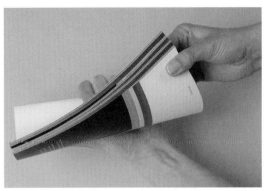

2010
Identity for the Spanish
Laus Design Awards.

2012
Lamp created in
collaboration with
Entresuelo1a for
the exhibition 'Poñer
Cousas en Orde'.

2012
Lamp created in
collaboration with
Entresuelo1a for
the exhibition 'Poñer
Cousas en Orde'.

2014
Identity design for
Estampaciones Fuerte,
a metal stamping
company.

The main objective was to design a new, modern identity for this metal stamping company. The identity needed to reflect the company's values in a straightforward way, at the same time as showing the technical side of the business.

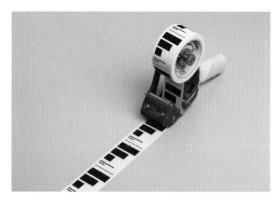
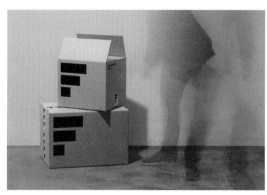
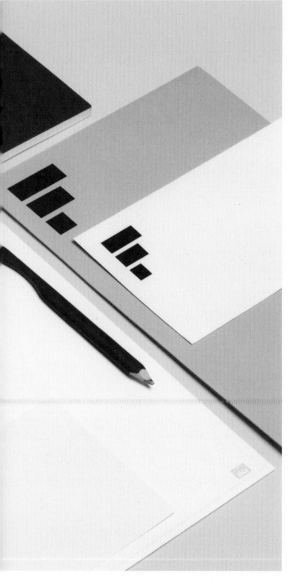

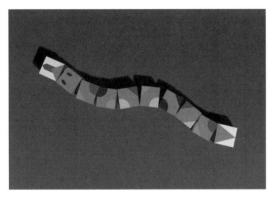

10 blocks 6 puzzles

2018
Puzzle illustration
for PAP YAY.

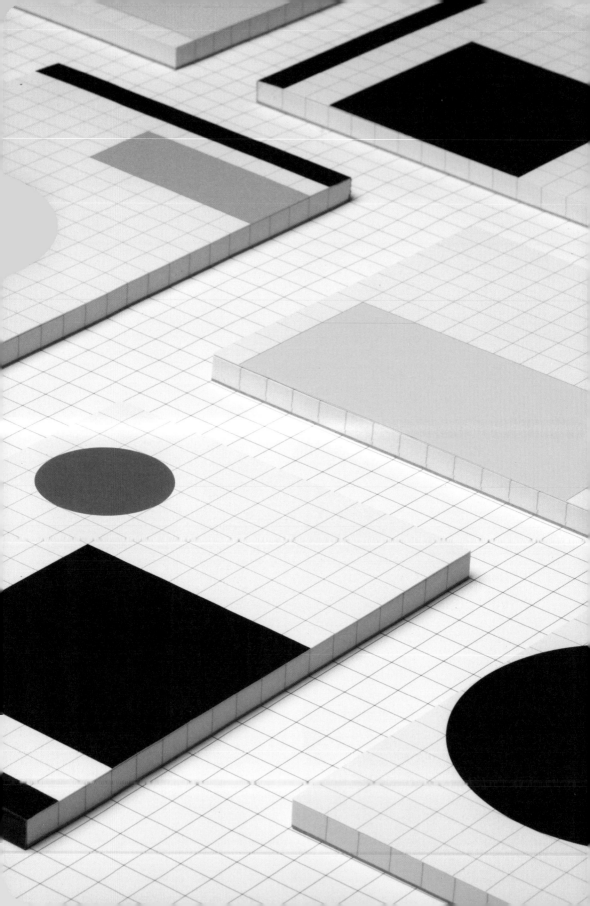

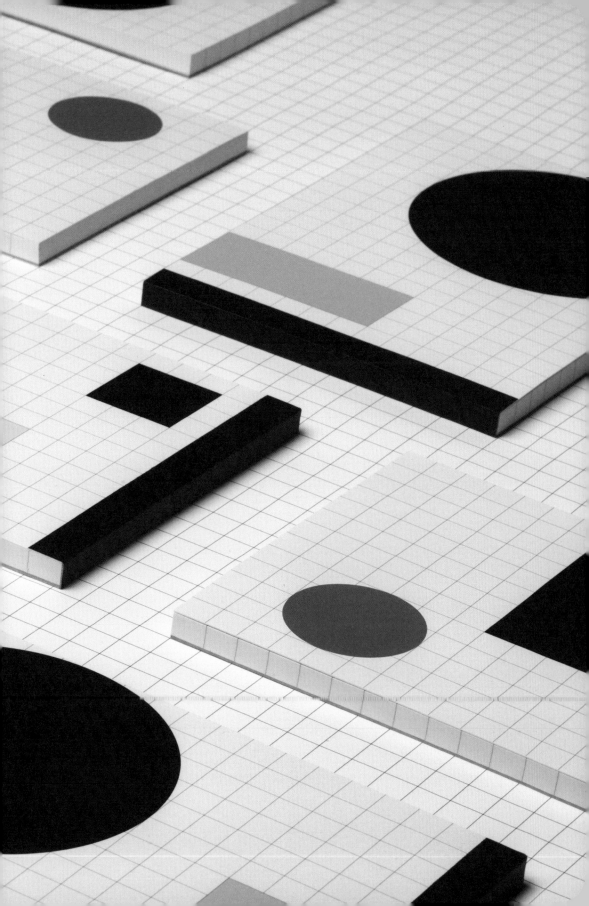

rebuild japan

← 2011
Wallpaper design
for Rebuild Japan's
WallForJapan app
to raise funds for
the tragedy that hit
the country in 2011.

2015
Poster designed for
Coca-Cola to celebrate
100 years of their iconic
bottle design.

2013
Self-promotional
Christmas poster
for Hey.

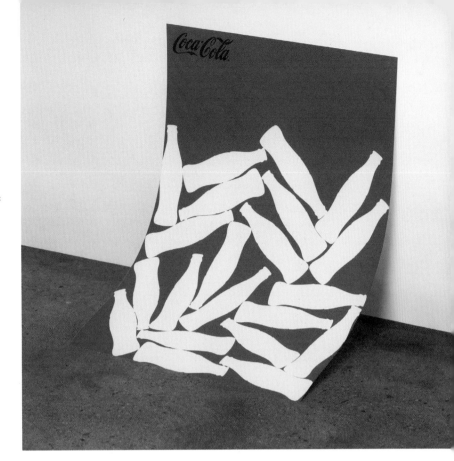

2019
Five posters designed
for Work & Co., an
agency developing digital
products for brands.

Cruz Roja Española

2016

Red Cross is the world's largest humanitarian network. They work to meet the needs and improve the lives of vulnerable people.

The goal of this project was to communicate the seven Red Cross values through a series of posters. The campaign, which grew out of a children's workshop at the El Pinar youth centre in Loja, needed to reflect the social character of Red Cross as well as the experiences of the participants during the activity.

The illustrations for the posters came from the creative work the children themselves produced in the workshop. Their drawings were selected, edited and vectors were applied to arrive at powerful and effective results. Both design and copy gave the campaign a context and a childlike voice. The invented quotes, alongside the images, allowed Hey to explain, in a simple and educational way, Red Cross's seven core values: Humanity, Impartiality, Neutrality, Independence, Voluntary service, Unity and Universality.

The aim of the campaign was not only to communicate the client's values and their mission but also to generate empathy and raise awareness. Hey's challenge was to convey a large amount of serious and complex information, using just a few tools and resources.

The goal of this project was
to spread the seven Red
Cross values through a series
of posters.

2016
Series of posters for
Cruz Roja Española.

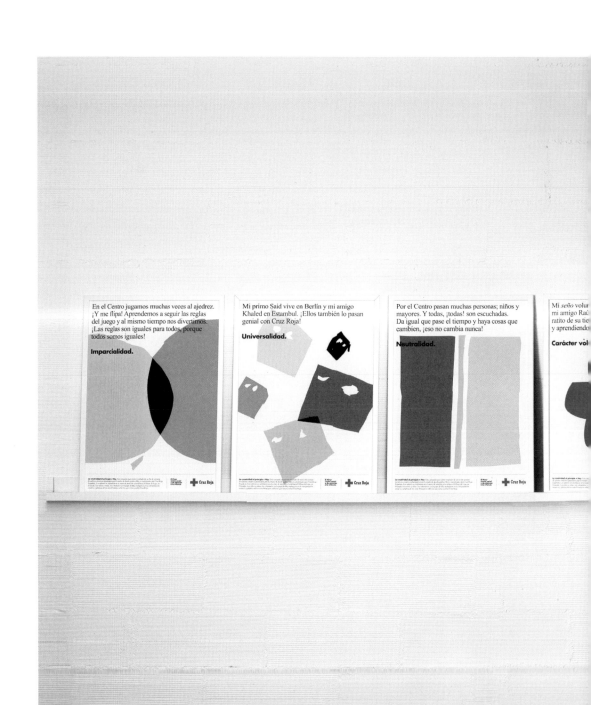

The illustrations for the posters came from the creative work the children themselves produced in the workshop. Their drawings were selected, edited and vectors were applied to arrive at powerful and effective results.

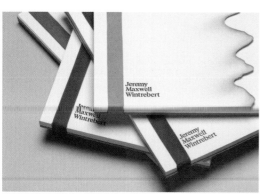
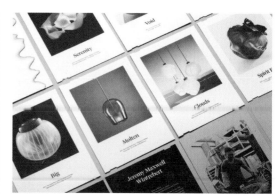

Jeremy Maxwell Wintrebert

2014

The starting point of this project was Hey's wish to genuinely share with people what being a modern glassblower really means. The studio wondered how to communicate the spirit of the work beyond the usual photography of the final pieces.

Even though the works have to speak for themselves, there was still a desire to unveil the story behind the making of the pieces. Hey's aim was to share glimpses of the creative process and of the daily life within the workshop, adding further insight into the process.

The identity is simple yet elegant with a white, black and kraft paper colour palette. Textures win over colours and the details are references to the handmade nature of the objects.

Hey imagined the laser-burned pattern as, 'a border for creativity'. It also gives a hint of the intense heat inside the workshop. The burned paper even smells like the folded newsprint which is used as a tool to shape the hot glass.

2014
Identity for a
glassblowing artist.

People & Places

2012
A series of illustrations
titled 'Hey Characters',
which formed a book
of the same name.

PayPal

2016

PayPal, the company that gives people around the world more direct control over their money, asked the global design boutique Mucho in San Francisco to define their new illustration style. Under the creative direction of Mucho, Hey worked on a range of illustrated stories which showed PayPal as customer-champions. They wanted to convey the ideas of 'networks', 'global inclusion' and the perceived tension between 'innovation' and 'heart and soul'.

Hey's challenge was to find a way to visualise the stories, without being clichéd. Their solution was a long, linear illustrative style.

Hey made several conceptual, heroic poster illustrations which were made up of different, but connected, individual icons. Both the resulting illustrations and all the individual icons symbolise the concept behind each story. Hey's conceptual illustrations have been applied across PayPal's USA web pages.

Hey's challenge was to find a way to visualise the stories, without being clichéd. Their solution was a long, linear illustrative style.

2016 ↗
Illustrations for PayPal.

2014
Illustrations in
collaboration with
'El País' for the
technology section
of its Sunday magazine
'El País semanal'.

TECNOLOGÍA

El autorretrato de la era digital es el 'selfie'. Solo a Instagram se han subido 90 millones de fotos con el 'hashtag' #Me. La pose suele ser la siguiente: mano estirada para alejar la cámara, primer plano a la cara y morritos para la posteridad. Es un divertimento. El proceso es simple, rápido y adictivo. Se creía que era un fenómeno adolescente hasta que Hillary Clinton y Meryl Streep publicaron el suyo. POR *Karelia Vázquez*

Territorio Instagram. Era zona natural de los *selfies*, pero la llegada de Snapchat, un servicio de mensajería que autodestruye las imágenes a voluntad del autor, ha seducido rápidamente a la cultura *selfie*. El 70% de sus usuarios, según Evan Spiegel (CEO de Snapchat), son mujeres. Para un *sexting* sin rastro.

Más que vanidad. "La gente lucha por entender qué imagen tiene ante los otros", dice Clive Thompson, autor del libro *Smarter than you think. How technology is changing our minds for better*". En agosto pasado, el diccionario de Oxford admitió el término y lo nombró palabra del año.

Naturalidad, pero con filtros. Para algunos observadores, como la psicóloga Sarah J. Gervais, este tipo de capturas son una rebelión contra las fotos perfectas y retocadas, de gesto lánguido y postura imposible. Aunque haya filtros. "En Instagram, la gente ha tomado el poder, y hasta muchos famosos se muestran de un modo más natural", dice la especialista.

Pioneros. Los *selfies* (un diminutivo de autorretrato, en inglés) aparecieron en 2004 en Flickr. Fue la llegada de los *smartphones*, concretamente el iPhone 4 con su cámara frontal, lo que los hizo un fenómeno viral. Según una encuesta reciente del Pew Research Center, más del 90% de los adolescentes estadounidenses los publican regularmente.

Explosión 'single'. Su éxito se ha visto favorecido por la mayor calidad de las cámaras en teléfonos y porque hay más solteros y divorciados que nunca. Gente que vive y viaja sola. No siempre tienen a alguien que les tome una foto y quieren documentar gráficamente sus viajes y su vida.

Frente a frente. Verse las caras refuerza los lazos sociales. "Nuestro cerebro está diseñado para procesar más rápido la imágenes y se implica más cuando ve un rostro. En un álbum se recuerdan mejor los primeros planos y los autorretratos", explica Pamela Rutledge, directora de Media Psychology Research Center.

TRAZANDO LA HISTORIA **2005** Se usa por primera vez el término *selfie* en un tutorial de fotografía de Richard Krause. **2007** Un usuario de Flickr crea el grupo Selfie Shots y define la palabra como "un autorretrato que uno se hace con el brazo extendido". **Junio de 2010** Llega el iPhone 4. **Octubre de 2010** Llega Instagram. **Diciembre de 2012** La revista *Time* la incluye entre las palabras de moda del año: "Puede hacerse desde cualquier ángulo e incluye siempre una parte del brazo del fotógrafo". **Enero de 2013** Las hijas de Barack Obama, Malia y Sasha, son fotografiadas mientras se hacían un *selfie* en la toma de posesión de su padre. **Marzo de 2013** The Oxford English Dictionary... **Noviembre de 2013** El Diccionario de Oxford la nombra palabra del año.

Controlar el 'smartphone' antes que el lápiz. Un 70% de los niños manejarán con soltura una tableta antes de ir a la escuela. El mundo se divide entre padres que creen que sus retoños deben interactuar cuanto antes con el mundo y otros que se dedican a proteger a su prole de Internet. Algunos estudios aseguran que la postura de los padres influye poco en las preferencias de los niños, que mantienen sus prácticas contra viento y marea. POR *Karelia Vázquez*

Del juguete al móvil.
Un 25% de niños españoles de entre 8 y 12 años prefieren que le regalen un teléfono a un juguete, según los datos que aporta la organización El Chupete. Casi un 40% de los niños mayores de 13 años tiene un móvil de última generación. En Estados Unidos, a los 8 años la mitad de los niños ya usa 'smartphones' y tabletas.

Lluvia de mensajes.
Entre 60 y 100 mensajes (en el caso de las chicas) es lo que llegan a intercambiar los niños y adolescentes en un solo día. Los servicios de mensajería instantánea, como Whatsapp o Snapchat están entre sus preferidos. Ahí es donde tiene lugar buena parte de su vida social.

¿Aprendió a hablar o a usar la tableta?
Dos de cada cinco niños han utilizado una tableta antes de ser capaces de pronunciar una frase completa, según un informe de la organización Common Sense Media, que afirma que el 38% de los niños menores de dos años utiliza un dispositivo móvil para jugar, ver vídeos o para otros fines. Una cifra que hace tan solo dos años no superaba el 10%.

Planeta efímero.
Snapchat les encanta a los adolescentes porque no deja huellas de sus andanzas digitales. Las fotos y vídeos compartidos se autodestruyen, por tanto no se pueden almacenar ni reenviar a otro terminal. La persona que envía el contenido puede seleccionar los segundos de vida del mensaje antes de que desaparezca definitivamente. Se dice que es una aplicación pensada para el 'sexting' y otros juegos.

Televisión o tableta.
Aunque el amor por la caja tonta se mantiene firme y estable en sus corazones, el uso de dispositivos móviles para consumir contenidos audiovisuales creció del 4% al 10% entre 2011 y 2013, frente a la caída del DVD. Un avance significativo.

El triple de tiempo.
Los niños de 0 a 8 años pasaron 15 minutos diarios con algún 'gadget' en 2013. Mientras que en 2011 solo le dedicaban cinco minutos. Como consecuencia, dicen desde Common Sense Media, niños que aún no hablan caminan hasta la pantalla de un televisor e intentan interactuar con él como si fuera una tableta o un teléfono.

LA REVISTA 'CHILDHOOD EDUCATION' sostiene que existe mucha mitología alrededor de los niños y la tecnología. Para demostrarlo publica un estudio que desmonta el mito por excelencia: los niños son 'per se' nativos digitales. La investigación, firmada por Lydia Plowman y Joanna McPake, demuestra que entre los tres y cuatro años muchos niños no están cómodos con la tecnología y creen que usar un ordenador es "difícil". Aunque las tabletas han mejorado mucho esta relación, las investigadoras insisten en que los niños no comprenden del todo el diseño de las 'interfaces' de Internet, ni siquiera en el caso de los juegos. Todo lo que hacen es imitarlo a usted. Pero esta es solo una de las tantas teorías que existen sobre el asunto, si usted prefiere creer que su hijo será el próximo Bill Gates, habrá algún otro estudio que se lo confirme.

2015
Cover design for
'Brummel' magazine.

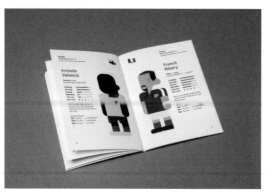

2014
Illustration of 32 football
players for a book titled
'Gol', in collaboration
with Studio DBD,
for TwentyTwentyTwo.

Ensaimadart

2012

To celebrate its 50th anniversary, Amadip Esment launched a project to create new label designs for Ensaimada boxes. This traditional, popular cake from the island of Majorca comes in distinctive octagonal boxes, onto which the circular design is printed.

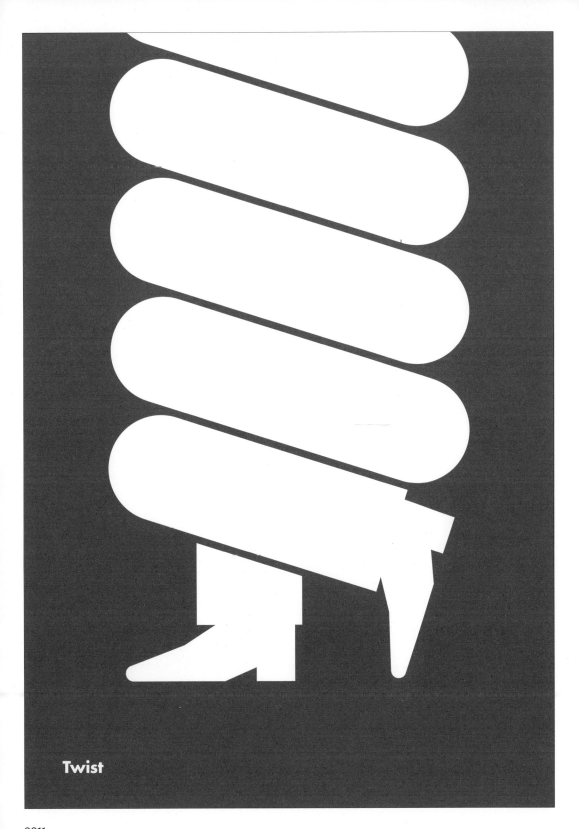

Twist

2011
Poster for the music genre
'twist' for Edits by Edit.

2013
Illustrations for
an exhibition titled
'Oh My God'.

Microsoft Lumia

2014

Microsoft Lumia launched the #MakeItHappen campaign to help motivate people to stick to their New Year's resolutions. Hey was one of five studios and illustrators asked to create a set of images for the project.

Users simply shared their resolution, chose an artist and created their own artwork. This could then be used as a screensaver or printed out and stuck on the fridge door, giving people a little, visible reminder of their goals for the new year.

EveryHey

2014–2015

EveryHey started on Instagram (@every_hey) at the beginning of 2014 and at that time an account where the topic was illustration wasn't very common. The project included 400 illustrations of public figures from popular culture – from singers and sports stars to works of art, also taking in the heroes and villains of films, books, comics and TV programmes.

   The project culminated in an exhibition and the publication, in English, of a limited-edition book containing all the illustrations which also hoped to explain a little more about how and why they were made. The book 'EveryHey' was used as a way to explain the technical and theoretical elements of this very distinct type of illustration.

   These 400 characters moved from digital form onto paper, both in the book and in the exhibition Hey organised titled 'EveryHey, Just People by Hey' in October 2015 at The Folio Club, Barcelona.

   The three week exhibition brought the project to an end and took a look at four hundred reinterpreted figures from popular culture. Only one poster of each character was on sale during the three week exhibition at The Folio Club.

The project included 400 illustrations of public figures from popular culture – from singers and sports stars to works of art, also taking in the heroes and villains of films, books, comics and TV programmes.

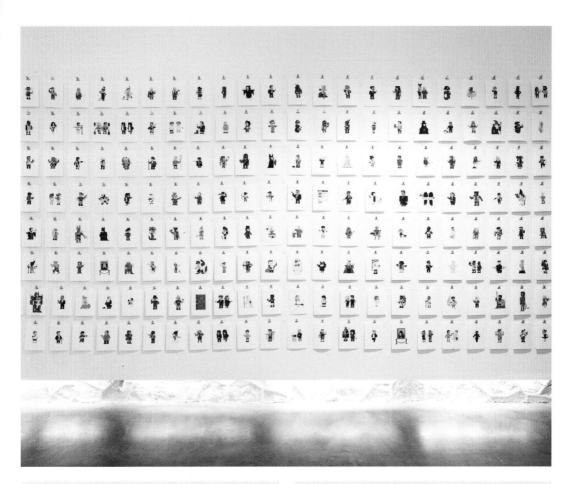

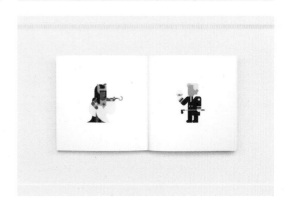

2014–2015
Instagram feed,
exhibition and book,
titled 'EveryHey'.

The three week exhibition brought the project to an end and took a look at four hundred reinterpreted figures from popular culture. Only one poster of each character was on sale during the three week exhibition at The Folio Club.

2010
Illustrations designed
for a collective
exhibition titled 'Loft
is in the Air' by Sucre.

2017
Wall murals for UNIQLO
stores, depicting
activities and things
the people of Barcelona
do in their free time.

2019
Wall murals for UNIQLO'S
La Diagonal store.

Uniqlo approached Hey to illustrate a hero mural in La Diagonal, Barcelona. Busy, dynamic and cosmopolitan, the diagonal is the artery of Barcelona, one of the largest and most important avenues in the city and this mural reflects this.

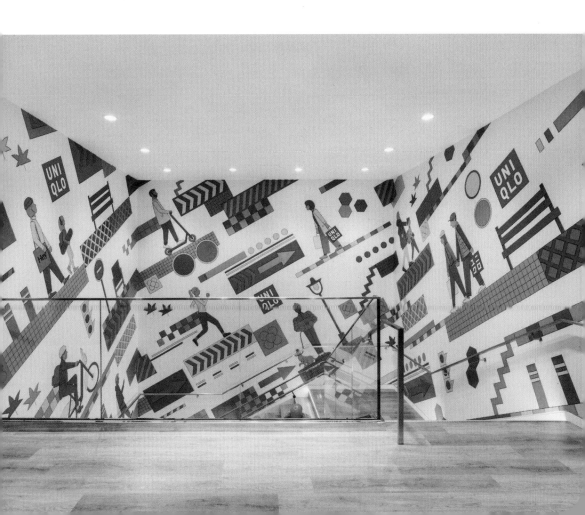

2015
Poster design for
Glug, in collaboration
with the United
Nations, representing
good health – a UN
developmental goal.

2015
'January' poster
for HeyShop.

2014
'August' poster
for HeyShop.

2014
'Sea Stripes' poster
for HeyShop.

2019 ↗
Illustrations for BlackBird,
a flight sharing app.

Three

2014

Three, the telecoms company, asked Hey to help brighten up their new offices in Dublin. They used three letter words to name all their meeting rooms and Hey made illustrations for them to give each room a unique and fun feel. The words were all very different. The studio were given 'Hen, Hex, Hot, Hue, Ice, Joy, Kit, Kob, Koi' and 'Lab' to illustrate.

2014
Office murals for Three.

2014
Illustrated campaign, in
collaboration with SCPF
agency, for San Miguel.

Under the slogan 'A Place Called the World' and connecting the San Miguel brand with Athletic Club de Bilbao, Hey illustrated a map of the world where the football club's fans take over in their distinctive Basque clothes.

Search TfL Journey Planner
Now with more cycling
and walking routes

MAYOR OF LONDON

↖ 2016
Poster for Transport
for London, to promote
the WiFi connections
in London underground
stations.

2012
Cover illustration
for Process Journal.

2010
Illustration and icon
design for Nokia,
commissioned
by DesignStudio.

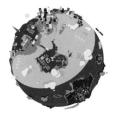

2010
Illustration and icon
design for Nokia,
commissioned
by DesignStudio.

Hey

2015
Illustration for a self-promotional Christmas poster.

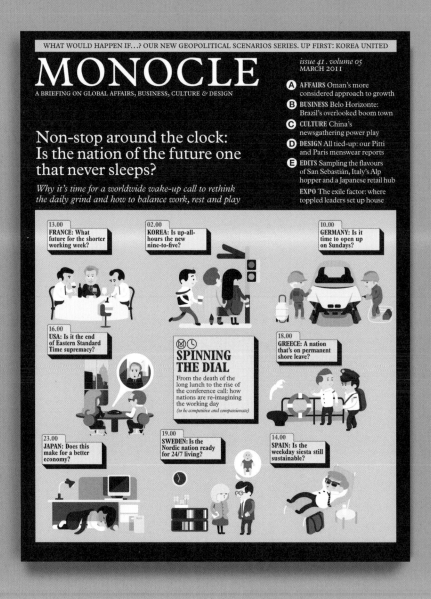

2013
Editorial illustrations
for 'Monocle' magazine.

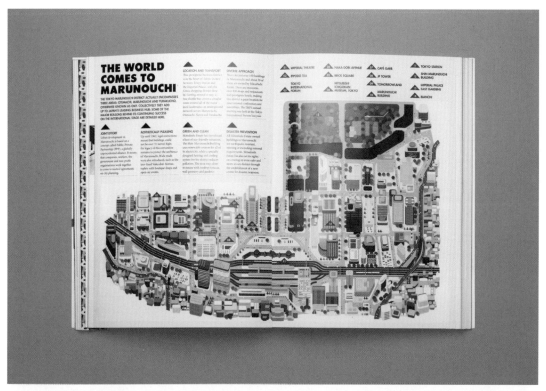

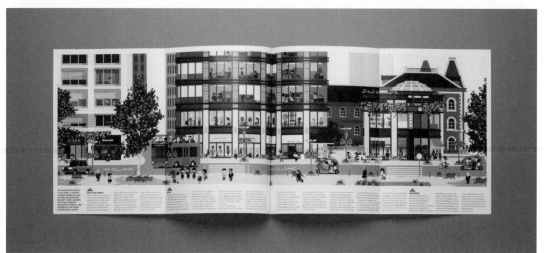

Typography

SO
aceite de oliva virgen extra
SOLO
aceite de oliva virgen extra
arbequina
SOL
aceite de oliva virgen extra

ArtFad

2011–2014

Hey have created a number of graphic identities for ArtFad, the Contemporary Art and Craft Awards. Their first identity, designed in 2011, was hand-stamped which resulted in each invitation being unique, with no two the same.

This hand-crafted approach was explored further in subsequent campaigns. For instance, the 2012 edition took the graphic language of tape to convey, 'parallel paths between art and craft'. The studio made 500 hand-made invitations – the only machinery process was the printing of text – resulting in each invitation having a different colour scheme and appearance.

In the 2014 edition, the studio's idea was to represent a geometrical 'A' in the layout as an outline. Colour, patterns and materials where then added, to create the final appearance. The invitations were made using 100 different Maxon comic patterns, which Hey applied manually, one by one.

The first identity, designed in 2011, was hand-stamped which resulted in each invitation being unique, with no two the same.

2011 ↗
Identity design
for ArtFad.

2011
Identity design
for ArtFad.

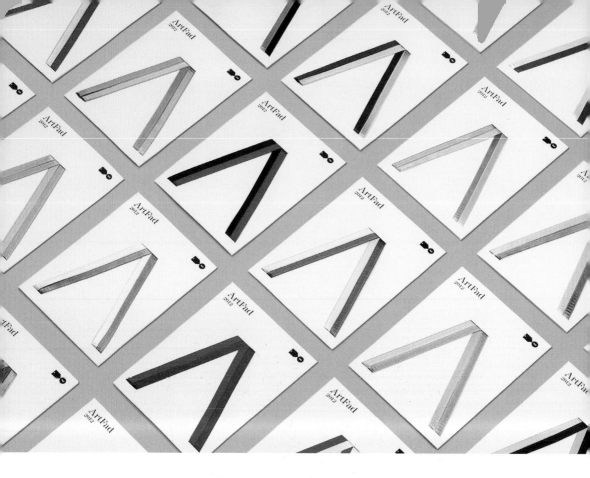

The 2012 edition took the graphic language of tape to convey parallel paths between art and craft. The studio made 500 hand-made invitations – the only machinery process was the printing of text.

2012
Identity design
for ArtFad.

2013
Identity design
for ArtFad.

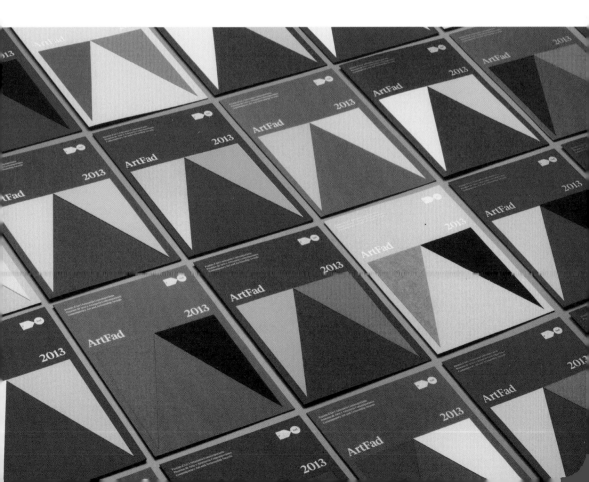

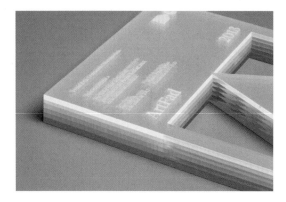

2013
Identity design
for ArtFad.

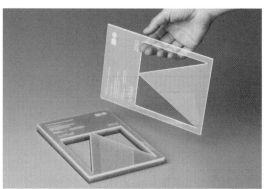

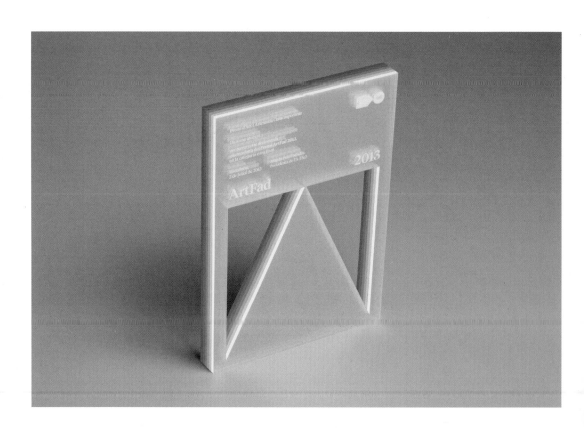

In the 2014 edition, the studio's idea was to represent a geometrical 'A' in the layout as an outline. Colour, patterns and materials where then added, to create the final appearance.

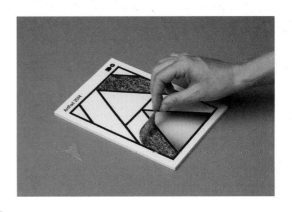

2014
Identity design
for ArtFad.

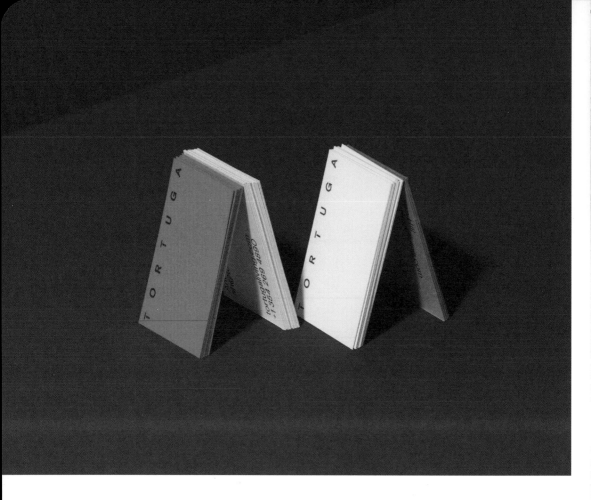

The name Tortuga (Turtle) was
the starting point for this identity.
It gave the branding meaning and
the main idea came from there.
The logotype is alive; its movement
suggests the calmly determined
way turtles move through the water.

2019
Identity and packaging
design for Tortuga,
a furniture company.

TORTUGA

Pyramid Bracket

tortugaliving.com

TORTUGA

Pyramid Bracket

tortugaliving.com

Mallorca
Lanzarote
Ibiza
Tenerife
Menorca

Te invitamos a conocer las mejores ofertas de
nuestro país. Unas vacaciones perfectas para
pasar las mejores vacaciones.

B the travel brand

California

945€

5 días / 4 noches
Vuelo + Hotel
Puente de Diciembre

B the travel brand

Mallorca, Ámsterdam
París, Madrid, Oporto
Roma, Granada, Praga
Londres, Berlín, Viena
Reikiavik, Edimburgo
Estambul, Budapest
Zúrich, Venecia, Lisboa
Estocolmo, Atenas.

B the travel brand

2015
Graphic identity
for the travel agency
B the travel brand.

2019 →
Identity for Cloudworks,
a co-working space
provider.

Lisboa

287€

B the travel brand

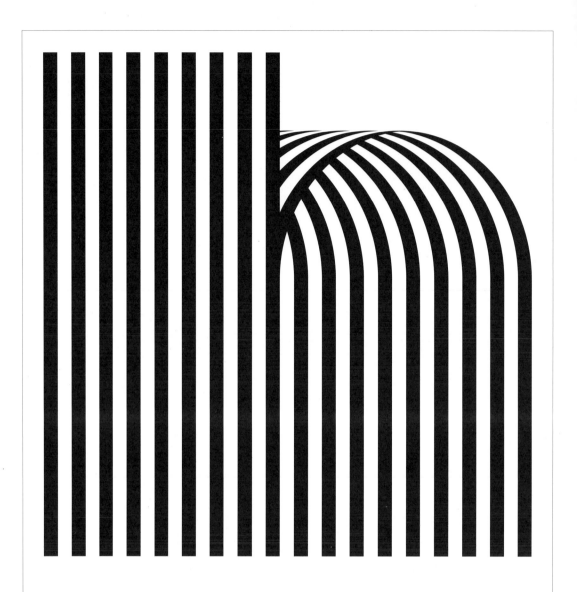

2014
'H' poster for HeyShop.

2013
'Berlin & Barcelona' poster
for the 'ReciproCity' exhibition.

2009
Poster designs for
Intermón Oxfam.

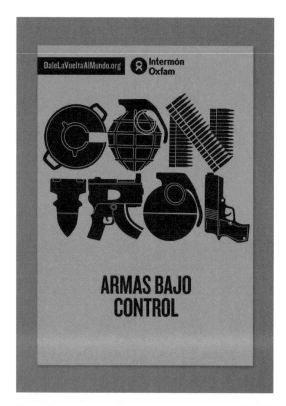

BUSCAMOS
UNIVERSITARIOS

2015
Notebook design
for HeyShop.

The Designers Foundry

2016

The Designers Foundry (TDF) is an international team of type designers. They strive to provide designers from all backgrounds with a quality resource of curated fonts.

To celebrate their fourth anniversary, TDF approached Hey to design a special poster to mark the occasion. The result is a silver foiled '4' print which references TDF's digital products and team of designers, who have been working around the clock, in different time zones, for the past four years.

A limited number of these artworks were produced in four different colours on high quality paper for TDF's customers.

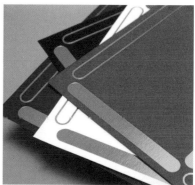

2016
Posters designed
for TDF.

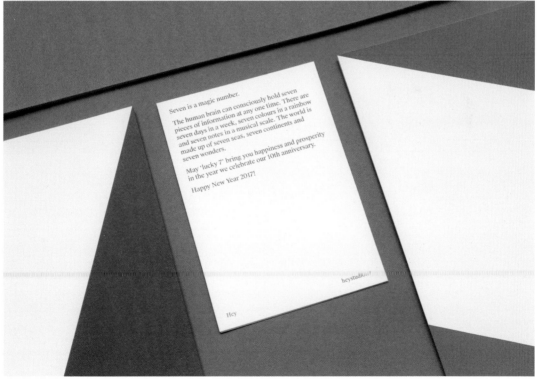

Seven is a magic number.

The human brain can consciously hold seven pieces of information at any one time. There are seven days in a week, seven colours in a rainbow and seven notes in a musical scale. The world is made up of seven seas, seven continents and seven wonders.

May 'lucky 7' bring you happiness and prosperity in the year we celebrate our 10th anniversary.

Happy New Year 2017!

Hey

heystudio117

2016
New year celebratory
posters for 2017.

2014
New Year celebratory
print for 2015.

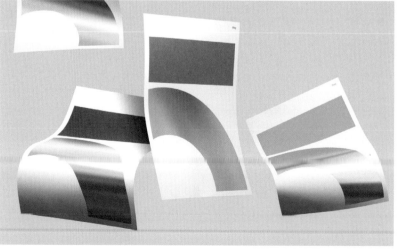

Sophie Nguyen Arc

SN^A

SN^A

SN^A

NA

uyen
RIBA DPLG

estern Studios
Road, London W2 5EU
0 3176 6165
7 1783 4448

phienguyenarchitects.com
yenarchitects.com

uyen

Lumik

2016

Lumik is a lighting design and manufacturing company with more than 65 years of experience behind it. Founded in Barcelona in 2016, it is the result of a partnership between the traditional metalworking company run by brothers Francesc and Ferran Martí and interior designer and art director, Frank Domínguez.

Inspired by the latest trends and particularly by the needs of its customers, Lumik required a visual identity that reflected both its trendsetter character, as well as its made-on-demand nature.

The result is a visual identity based on numerous colours that reflects all the possibilities the brand offers to its clients by creating customised lighting.

The specially designed typography is a stencil font that symbolises individual LED light sticks.

2016
Visual identity designed
for Lumik.

Ferran Martí

Santiago ...
Pol. Ind. C...
08213 Polin...
T 937 131 166
M 649 947 113
lumik.es

LUMIK

LUMIK

LUMIK

Santiago Rusiñol 14, nave B5
Pol. Ind. Can Humet de Dalt
08213 Polinyà, Barcelona
937 131 166
lumik.es

hola@lumik.es

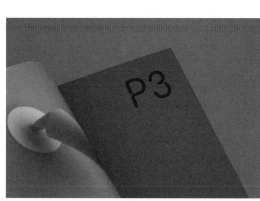

Solo

2020

Solo is an extra virgin olive oil from an extraordinary place – Baños de la Encina, in the province of Jaén, one of the most renowned olive oil producing regions in the world.

As the name suggests, Solo stands for simplicity and purity. Inspired by the belief that when things are created locally, fairly and without a rush, the rewards are much greater.

Siblings Ana and Juan started this project as a homage to their grandfather who spent his whole life nurturing the ancient olive fields.

Drawing upon this rich history and tradition, Hey wanted to showcase the oil by creating a series of organic textures that highlight what's inside the bottle. The designs also help differentiate each variety of olive.

By combining this powerful palette with a striking typeface and bold packaging, they aimed for a high-end look to ensure the product stands out in the world of olive oil.

As the name suggests, Solo stands for simplicity and purity. Inspired by the belief that when things are created locally, fairly and without a rush, the rewards are much greater.

2020
Identity and packaging
design for Solo, an
extra virgin olive oil.

Sebinta's services aim to inspire optimism and trust, as well as spark conversation towards positive change in people's lives and careers. To develop the brand, Hey relied on the concept of 'Bringing a smile to people's faces'. The result is a visual identity that sparks positivism, fun and enthusiasm.

2020
Identity for Sebinta,
a Corporate Stress
Management &
Efficiency Consultants.

2018 →
Business card design
for Iley.

↖ 2020
'Hey Ale Paul' poster,
designed in collaboration
with Ale Paul for HeyShop.

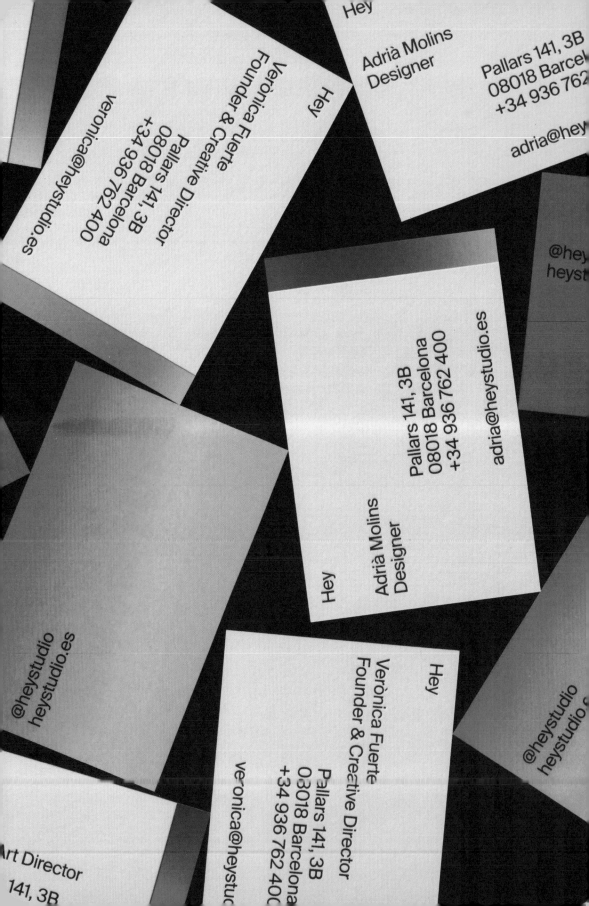

Adrià Molins
Designer

Pallars 141, 3B
08018 Barcelona
+34 936 762 400

adria@heystudio.es

Hey

Adrià Molins
Designer

Pallars 141, 3B
08018 Barcelona
+34 936 762 400

adria@heystudio.es

Hey

Adrià Molins
Designer

Pallars 141, 3B
08018 Barcelona
+34 936 762 400

adria@heystudio.es

Hey

Gemma Faja
HeyShop Man

Pa
08
+34 9

gemma@

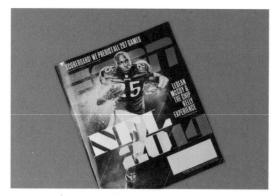

2014
Display typeface,
commissioned
by 'ESPN' magazine
for an NFL issue.

2015 →
Lettering for 'ESPN'
magazine's 'Forward'
section.

Kosmopolis

2017

Kosmopolis is a biennial literature festival that has been organised by the Centre de Cultura Contemporània de Barcelona since 2002. The duration of the festival itself is five days but an ongoing programme keeps the spirit of the event alive all year round. The event promotes a concept of 'amplified literature' in many different forms and brings together different types of professionals to discuss the key issues that concern literature today.

Hey was commissioned to visually rebrand Kosmopolis, as well as to work on the identity and communication campaign for the 2017 edition.

In keeping with the visual identity of past editions, Hey decided to establish red as the main colour but also created a specially made typeface – since words are the essence of the festival and they wanted to give the text used in communications more character.

Hey came up with a typeface based on the multidisciplinary nature of the festival. It was applied to the logo, the short version logo for each edition (the K plus the year) and other display applications. Each character was created according to common parameters. The studio then customised the stroke on some of them. Each stroke intervention directly refers to a specific use of the word: digital words, hand-written words and painted words. This made-to-measure typeface gave the festival both personality and a brand image.

For the 2017 communications campaign, Hey worked on a visual concept from the strategic communications agency Usted. They created an icon series that brought together pictograms of different styles to reinforce the varied nature of the festival.

Hey came up with a typeface based on the multidisciplinary nature of the festival.

2017 ↗
Identity for literature
festival Kosmopolis.

KOSMOPOLIS
La literatura és viva.
Es pot llegir, escriure,
filmar, cantar...

Live Out Festival

2016

Live Out, the indie pop-rock music festival of Monterrey, Mexico, asked Hey to design its campaign for 2016.

The goal of this edition was to transmit 'freshness'. They wanted to make a difference and stand out nationally in their sector – at the same time as emphasising their position as a respected music festival.

Hey created a bold and strong identity, based on a geometric, block layout. Bold, coloured, capital letters are the main feature of the visual communication. The design is flexible and allows for the creation of different pieces, with the information easily being substituted and updated as required.

2016
Visual identity for Live
Out music festival.

Biblioteca Universal Empúries

RICARD SOLÉ
XARXES
COMPLEXES
DEL GENOMA A INTERNET

Biblioteca Universal Empúries

DANIEL
PENNAC
MAL
D'ESCOLA

Biblioteca Universal Empúries

JOSEP-ANTON
FERNÀNDEZ
EL MALESTAR
EN LA CULTURA
CATALANA

Biblioteca Universal Empúries

SLAVOJ
ŽIŽEK
VIOLÈNCIA

Biblioteca Universal Empúries

AHMED RASHID

AUTOR D'«ELS TALIBANS»

DESCENS AL CAOS

Els Estats Units i el fracàs de la construcció nacional al Pakistan, l'Afganistan i l'Àsia Central

MEMORIAL

CAPITAL COMMENT

TASTE

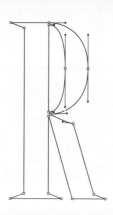

CHARACTER

2015
Typeface for the front
cover of 'Washingtonian'
magazine.

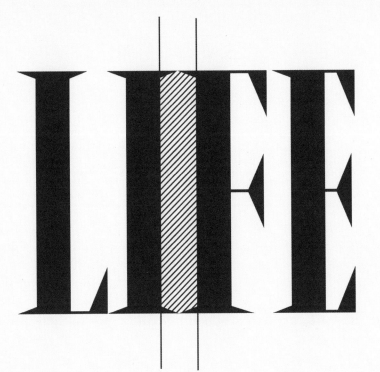

WHERE & WHEN

HOME

Have a Great Day Films

2015

Jérôme de Gerlache is the French filmmaker behind this production company which makes documentaries and feature films. Gerlache has a taste for professional risk-taking, with a very special and distinct way of making short films, advertisements and TV comedies.

His work's personality needed to be reflected within the brand's identity, which was to have a very clear message of 'positivity'. The brief was to create a forward looking, future-focused brand but also to place value on experience and authenticity.

This, along with a brand name with lots of different letters, led Hey to base the identity on a typographic approach which captured the essence of the cinema of old and the origins of movie storytelling. The logo plays with the arrangement of the words, which echoes classic cinema marquees.

This nod to the movie theatres of the last century is also continued with the colour palette. The yellow in the typography brings to mind back-lit lights. The logo can be put together in many different ways and it is easily converted into moving image, for use on film credits.

The logo plays with the arrangement of the words, which echoes classic cinema marquees.

2015 ↗
Identity for the production company Have a Great Day Films.

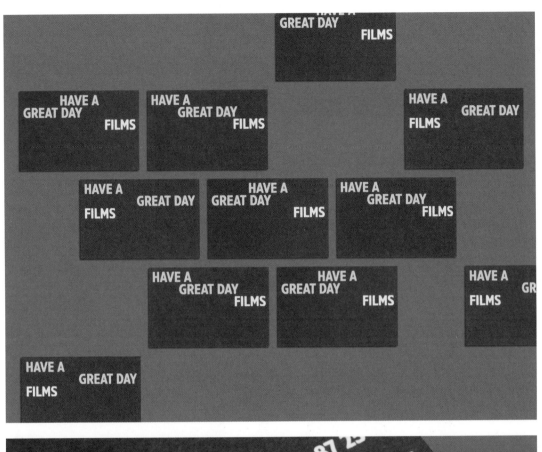

2014
'No Fly Posters' poster,
designed for Jon Bland.

2014 ↗
'Hello Bold Italic' poster,
celebrating the launch
of FS Emeric by Fontsmith.

Hello Bold *Italic*

Yeh

2017

'Yeh' was created by Hey to celebrate their first decade as a studio. It featured a brand new exhibition, as well as different creative activities that took place in November 2017, at the Montoya space in Barcelona.

'Yeh' is 'Hey' spelt backwards. It's a conceptual name, created by the communications agency Usted to highlight the studio's 10-year retrospective. The idea being that the studio were taking a look at themselves in a mirror and celebrating the history of Hey in reverse.

The exhibition included work Hey had created over the years which was displayed in a variety of formats, including original pieces and new installations.

Hey brought together new and old friends, clients, partners and sponsors in an event that included workshops, talks and screenings – all linked by their creativity. Professionals such as glass-blowing artist Jeremy Maxwell Wintrebert, illustrator Malika Favre, photographer Isabelita Virtual and natural cosmetics brand Mamita Botanical, all came to share their knowledge and inspire Yeh's guests.

2017
Ten year retrospective
of Hey's work titled 'Yeh'.

Hey 10th Anniversary retrospective

Exhibition, Workshops & Talks

9–11 November

Montoya C. Ávila 32 Barcelona

The exhibition included work Hey had created over the years which was displayed in a variety of formats which included original pieces and new installations.

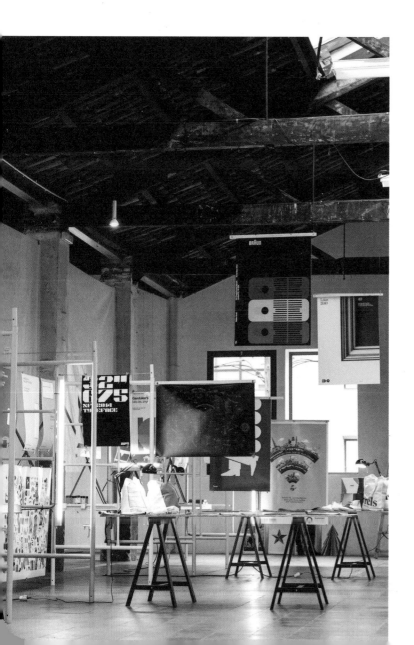

2017
Ten year retrospective
of Hey's work titled 'Yeh'.

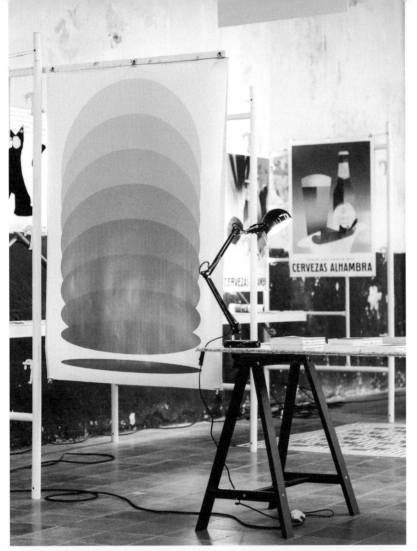

HeyShop

HeyShop

2019

In 2019 Hey took the next step on its journey and opened a shop in Barcelona. The shop showcases Hey products as well as collaborations with other brands, with creative direction by the studio. This is an evolution of the online shop it created in 2014, allowing it to carry on growing without creative limits.

The shop can be found at 4 Calle Doctor Dou in the Raval neighbourhood and invites visitors to immerse themselves in local design and explore Hey's universe of geometry, shapes and colours. It's a space that explains the studio's philosophy and promotes local talent, giving people an experience of the world of design.

HeyShop was conceived as an extension of the studio in Poblenou, which is why the different zones were designed to offer distinctive experiences to visitors, from the setting to the materials used, down to the smallest details that make the Hey style recognisable throughout. The space includes a café, a shop and a multipurpose area.

The shop invites visitors to immerse themselves in local design and explore Hey's universe of geometry, shapes and colours. It's a space that explains the studio's philosophy and promotes local talent.

2019 ↗
The HeyShop, located in Raval, Barcelona.

2019
The HeyShop, located
in Raval, Barcelona.

2020
'Hey Bag' design,
in collaboration
with Júlia Esqué.

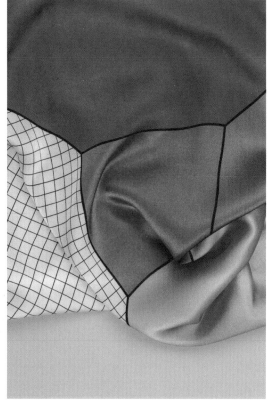

The FUGA Collection explores graphic compositions that play with the depth of enclosed spaces. The combination of formats and vanishing points allow each piece to be interpreted differently, making them at times familiar and others intriguing. A silk satin scarf, a high quality polyester wall-hanging and a woven cotton blanket make up this collection.

2020
Hey T-shirt, jumper,
hat and scarf designs.

↙ 2019
Packaging desing
for 'Hey Hola Coffee'.

2021
Limited edition of 10
handmade glass blown
marbles made in collab-
oration with Alex Trochut
and produced by The
Glass Apprentice.

Verònica Fuerte

CP Can you tell us about your upbringing? Where did you grow up?
Were you encouraged from a young age to go into a creative field?

VF I was born in Barcelona but my childhood was spent in a town not far outside the city. It was the type of small town where everyone knows each other, you walk to school and there's not really much to do when you are a teenager. From a very early age, as far as my memory stretches back, I was always interested in creativity. I remember that my after-school activities would always involve doing something like painting. This wasn't something my parents pushed on me because it wasn't really their world. Their background was industrial so they didn't come from a creative world and my brother was into sports, so I think this impulse must have come from me.

CP What first attracted you to graphic design?

VF Partly because of my upbringing, I wasn't really aware that graphic design existed, until it came to the time to decide what to study at university.

I went to one of those career fairs where you meet everybody and they explain the various course options. I remember that there was a stand where they explained about graphic design and I saw that there was a course module about colour. This amazed me! How could all that time just be about colour! I loved everything about colours, so straight away I was intrigued. At that stage I didn't know much more about graphic design but that was enough to get me interested. My first choice was actually to study film and I put graphic design second. Film was a very popular and competitive course, so I didn't get into that, so I studied graphic design instead.

CP Could you give us an idea of the background to you setting up Hey?
Did you have a vision for how you wanted your studio to be?

VF I had worked as an intern in a few different places while I was studying and when I finished I joined a big studio here in Barcelona. I stayed there a year and went on to work in four other studios over the following seven years. Having my own studio was always something I had wanted and at this point I decided I was ready to try it. Finding a style, my own style, and being able to work in a more aesthetic way were all part of the decision. To do this, I felt I had to stop working for other people. Finding the time and the energy make it impossible otherwise. A pause also gives you a chance to clear your head and think more clearly.

CP Where does the name Hey come from?

VF It wasn't a quick or easy process. I made lists and shortlists first. I wanted something that would work internationally and I was very sure that I didn't want to use my own name. Partly because I wanted something that sounded more contemporary and better reflected the type of studio I was trying to make. But also because, even though I was on my own when I started the studio, it could end up being more people than me. I have always found it strange and a bit unfair when people work under the name of the person who founded the company. It can make it seem like they lose something of their own personality when they are working. Hey won in the end as a name because it expressed an attitude more than anything else and I liked that. I had thought about 'Hola' as well because I liked its informality, its openness. Hey did this as well but it sounded more fun and relaxed. A friendly raised hand sort of greeting, rather than formally sticking out your hand to shake. This was the attitude that I wanted to represent the studio.

CP How did you find clients when you started out?

VF Like most people I survived at the start through friends. I had one client at the beginning, a friend of course. After a year I realised that I needed real clients, so I put together a portfolio and made a little book of the work I had done. I sent it out to museums, publishing houses and companies that I liked and admired. And I sent it to the correct person rather than a general address.

I spent time researching this, making follow-up calls and in the end I got responses. The financial crisis started not long after I set up, which changed a lot of things in Spain. One of its effects was the realisation that I had to look outside Spain for clients as well. In fact, one of these was Monocle magazine who came back, about six months later, asking for an illustration. This was great, as the readership of Monocle was exactly the type of people Hey needed to reach. Art directors read Monocle and that helps you to get known. While you need to be good to get clients, being lucky is arguably much more important and we have been lucky.

Social media has worked well for us, increasing our visibility. It's something that helps you connect with lots of people all over the world. It was a complete accident though, rather than a deliberate strategy. It just evolved. We started using different platforms, particularly Instagram, a few years in. In the beginning I signed up to a lot of these things just to get the Hey name before someone else. Some of them I started to play with but, I remember with Instagram that at the beginning I was just putting up personal things like photos of my daughter, with no idea of how to use it as a business tool.

CP　Where do you go for help and advice?

VF　The last few years I have realised that I needed to learn more about management and how to lead a company and so I hired a personal coach that helps me a lot. With Melisa, my coach, I'm able to improve and learn how to be a better leader, not only for myself but also for my team, with team coaching. It's not all about design, half of the things that happen at the studio are more about attitude, management, process and how to deal with our egos.

CP　Could you tell us about your working process?

VF　Our working process is not rigid but it follows the same form. The first contact is very important to have a better understanding of the client's needs. Colet, as the project manager, makes the first call and after that the creatives become involved. First we do our research to find out information that might help us understand the client better, as well as ideas and inspiration about what we could do for them. We will all come up with options and ideas which we share and discuss. From this we will usually select a few to present to the client. It's a collaborative approach which is something that works well in a small studio. Over time we have become much more efficient in how we work and good working processes certainly aid this.

CP　Can you give an example of how an outside collaboration might work?

VF　Because we are a small studio we are often collaborating with other people. Every time it is different because every project is unique. The first priority though is to look for collaborators who are the right fit for the client. However, it's also really important that they are good fit for us too. When you are collaborating, no matter in what way, it's important that you have the same vision and drive. One of the exciting things about working with other people is that you never really know where it will end up.

You need to keep an open mind when they come from different fields because their ideas will not always be what you had imagined at first. Above all, collaborating means meeting interesting people who have different skill sets and ways of looking at things and these encounters can often lead to unexpected ideas and solutions.

CP   How many of you are there now at Hey?

VF   At the studio in Poblenou there are five of us including me. Adrià, Sebastián and Marina are designers and Colet is the project manager. Then at the store we have Gemma, Zamira and Macari.

CP   Have you considered expanding your business further?

VF   My way of expanding the business is by taking on a variety of projects where there are no limits to creativity. It is not so much related to the size of the studio, I would prefer to keep that small and flexible.

Opening the physical store in 2019 was a way to expand the brand and make Hey more visible and accessible to everybody.

CP   What type of clients typically approach you and how do they benefit from working with a smaller studio?

VF   Our clients are varied. From museums and the city council in Barcelona to international brands like Uniqlo and Apple – they all share in common a desire for a unique, timeless and fresh creative approach for their companies. Startups often get in touch with us, not only because we have worked with big clients which reassures them, but also because we are small. It makes us more affordable than the bigger companies and more flexible. Everyone benefits because when it's a small team you have a much closer working relationship with the client and that is good for everyone.

　　　Our studio style obviously is also a part of this too. We describe our style as being fresh, bold and colourful. There's a directness to this which makes the message easy to understand. We have this kind of neutral, contemporary style and this is what some clients are looking for because it has a broader, more global appeal.

CP   Where do you draw inspiration from?

VF   There are artists and designers whose work I admire such as Saul Bass, Max Huber, Paul Rand and many more. They inspire not only for their work but for how they worked. Personally, I think that inspiration comes from constantly asking yourself questions. What are you doing, why are you doing it? As a studio our inspiration comes from anywhere and anything. Commercial work teaches you discipline and the need to be efficient, so inspiration has to be something you have a process for, so you don't waste time.

CP   Does living in Spain have any influence on your design aesthetic?

VF   Where you live has to affect the work you do. I am pretty sure that if I lived in, say London, that my aesthetic style would be different. As it is, I live in Barcelona, which I appreciate a lot. It's a vibrant city. It's a place where a lot of business gets done. All of these things influence your work and, if nothing else, they provide a pleasant working environment for you to get on with being creative. Our studio is located in Poblenou, an industrial area close to the centre that used to have a lot of factories. It still has industrial business but a lot of warehouse space has been converted for studios which has made it the creative hub of Barcelona. There are a lot of different people and businesses working here, which can lead to unexpected collaborations.

CP Do you have any issues maintaining the balance between creativity and profitability, or personal projects and client work?

VF Getting the right balance between personal projects and client work isn't hard because paying clients always have to come first. Without them there would be nothing else. Personal projects are for the times when you are less busy. Private projects are the chance to be more experimental and try out different approaches to things. None of this time is wasted because, apart from whatever personal satisfaction you gain from the project, it is also going to make your commercial work better. The commercial and the personal are connected and they feed into and off each other. The balance between creativity and profitability is something that I think you need to be more conscious of. Everyone wants to do fabulous creative projects all the time but they have to be profitable, otherwise you won't get many more chances. It's important to always be disciplined and efficient with your creativity but your work has to be good.

CP   What type of projects do you enjoy the most and what's the key
        to a successful outcome?
VF   The type of project is probably less important than the type of client.
We like projects where we can be more creative and where we have more
creative freedom. Creative freedom isn't wanting to be free from the
client but rather having a client who trusts you and works closely with you.
It should be a partnership and when you have a good working relationship
and understanding you achieve the best results.
CP   Do you have a dream client or collaborator in mind?
VF   We would like to work for a big, global brand on a large scale project.
We work for smaller companies a lot, so it would be exciting to work on
a larger scale. Technological companies are obviously appealing, because
you are working at the cutting-edge of business and you have a blanker
canvas to work with in many ways. I would also like to work more with fashion.
We haven't done a big, global logotype ever, so that is something that I would
like to have a chance to do one day.
        We have been lucky because we have already worked with a lot of
clients that a lot of people would list as dream clients. People like Nike,
Zalando and Coca-Cola. Any collaborator you work with, who brings you
a different way of seeing things, who takes you to unexpected, interesting
places, is what you dream of. As is anyone, client or collaborator, that you
make a good connection with.
CP   You've achieved so much already. What are your motivations for the
        future and is there something you particularly still want to do?
VF   Thinking of the future, I would love to be involve in even more high-
profile projects for bigger clients. I know that we've been working with very
prestigious clients but most of them are on small projects. We don't have the
same capacity as a big company and sometimes this is a boundary for that
kind of client.
        There are so many different types of clients and project out there
and we would be happy just to be able to experience as many as possible.
This is a motivation that keeps pushing you, because it is hard to get the
type of projects you have never done before. The desire is always to do
more things and to do them better and better. This can mean frustration
and disappointment as much as satisfaction and pleasure but the important
thing is always wanting to get better.

Client Index

Hey: Design & Illustration

© 2021 Counter-Print

Counter-Print
URL: counter-print.co.uk
Email: info@counter-print.co.uk

British Library cataloguing-in-publication data: A catalogue of this book can be found in the British Library.

ISBN: 978-0-9935812-7-4

First published in the United Kingdom in 2018 by Counter-Print.
Reprinted in 2021.

Colophon

Edited and produced by Counter-Print.

Design: Jon Dowling & Céline Leterme
Typefaces: Suisse Int'l
Printing and Binding: 1010 Printing International Limited

Hey
URL: heystudio.es
Email: hey@heystudio.es

Studio and portrait photography: Enric Badrinas & Martí Pujol

Project photography: All images are used with permission. Unless otherwise noted, project photography is by Roc Canals, Enric Badrinas and Martí Pujol.

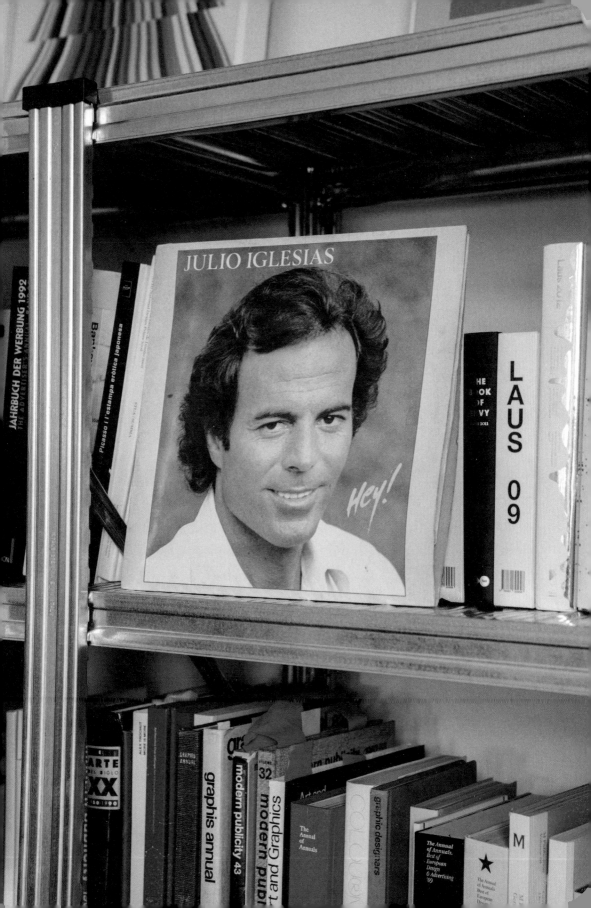